Tom Micha Finley Soan u

Hope this gives you.

Richard x ꞏ ꞏ/ꞏ ꞏꞏꞏꞏꞏꞏ

Keep Squeaking Through

The motivational maxims of Mortimer Mouse

Edited by

Richard Heller

© Richard Heller, 2023

Published by Xerus Publishing

All rights reserved. No part of this book may be reproduced, adapted, stored in a retrieval system or transmitted by any means, electronic, mechanical, photocopying, or otherwise without the prior written permission of the author.

The rights of Richard Heller to be identified as the author of this work have been asserted in accordance with the Copyright, Designs and Patents Act 1988.

© Illustrations by Amina Art Ansari

Cover design by Amina Art Ansari

A CIP catalogue record for this book is available from the British Library.

ISBN 978-1-8381654-1-3

Prepared and printed by:

York Publishing Services Ltd
64 Hallfield Road
Layerthorpe
York YO31 7ZQ

Tel: 01904 431213

Website: www.yps-publishing.co.uk

Of Mice And Me

When I first met Mortimer Mouse we were both at a low ebb. Indeed it was an ebb without the slightest sign of flow. I woke up in my flat in the building I call Rubato Towers after my style of piano playing, with an especially ghastly visit from the Mystery Virus (long before Covid) which I have named for a certain noxious British politician, whose name I cannot give away, as something unpleasant which keeps coming back. Its symptoms were not only physical (high temperature, aching everywhere, total torpor) but existential, sending a series of baleful messages. "Your life is worthless. You write novels that no one reads and screenplays nobody screens. Your published journalism, at its best, makes a passable litter tray for a rabbit with low standards. Your flat has been condemned as unfit for the neighbourhood termites."

Rubato Towers is a handsome building and my flat has been well adapted from it. But given my sentence as a writer to a life of indigent obscurity I had allowed it to decay. No one else would have wanted to live there. I realized this when I saw a mouse for the first time in my front room. He was selling The Big Issue.

That was Mortimer, although at that stage we did not get to first names.

I soon realized that he was a mouse of decided character and strong artistic judgments. After listening to only a few bars of me at the piano he criticised my tempi in "Love Letters In The Sand" by the legendary J Fred Coots. He left some songs of his own on the instrument. He told me he would have arranged them in my key if he knew what it was. He had had trouble getting his material published or even performed. I was not surprised after seeing the titles. The Mouse Of The Rising Sun. Mice Work If You Can Get Them. The Long And Winding Rodent. Squeak Low When You Squeak Love. And three Beatles covers: Please Cheese Me; Cheesy Woman; Cheese Loving Home.

He also gave me notes on my best screenplay, with a new role for a singing gerbil. He also proved to be an excellent watchmouse. Burglars came one night when I was away, but he told them that nothing was worth their bother. They did not take my silver, they polished it.

I discovered Mortimer's distinguished literary connexions when he suddenly did all the housework I had been neglecting. Then he asked me to replace two chairs in the drawing room and find something to cover the scorch marks on the settee. I asked why and he said that he was expecting an important visitor. Sure enough, a taller and more elegant rodent presented himself at Rubato Towers. He made a dramatic entrance, announced himself as the playwright Terence Ratagain and promptly fled to the nearest closet. He later emerged and gave readings from some of his famous plays: The Winslow Vole; Desperate Sables; The Deep Blue Cheese.

The success of Ratagain's visit led my lodger to make increasingly insensate demands. They included a bonsai rodentdendron plant, and a personal gym with an exercise wheel and an infinity pool in place of the settee. He also asked for a fancy wainscot: I told him he could make do with his old cardigan. He also wanted me to pour away all my stock of wine (supermarket Albanian red and white infuriator) and replace it with Mouse Cadet and Mouselle. I had to remind him that when he first appeared in my residence he was selling The Big Issue.

"I am expecting another important visitor," he replied, as loftily as a mouse can.

The second important visitor proved to be a sleek but etiolated chap about the same size as him with melancholy eyes peering over immaculate whiskers. He coughed delicately and my lodger introduced him proudly as "the novelist, Mousehole Proust." I offered the visitor refreshments but he refused anything more than a cup of weak herbal tea. This he stirred with a madeleine finger-biscuit from a packet he had brought himself. I thereupon made one of my very best jests: "I say, are you paddling madeleine home?" My goodness, how I roared! However, the two mice fixed me with a look such that I could have stored meat in it for several months. Eventually my lodger said "You are of course familiar with our guest's mousterpiece 'A La Recherche Du Temps Perdu', which I have translated a little freely as 'Now Where Did I Get Up To?' He is going to read us passages from the first three novels in the sequence: Swans Weigh More Than You Think; In The Shadow Of Young Squirrels In Blossom; Guernipigs Way."

The visitor began to recite, but I found myself asleep again long before he completed the subordinate clauses in his first sentence. I blamed the Mandelson Virus, (ooh what a giveaway!) but this did not prevent a serious rift between us. He cancelled his next visitor, whom he called "the distinguished absurdist, Albert Camouse", and stalked off in a huff to live with one of my neighbours who offered a better class of cheese.

His place as my lodger was taken by a cockroach called kafkaa. He was a poet like his more famous cousin archy, the vers libre bard celebrated for his life of mehitabel the cat. In imitation of his cousin, kafkaa announced himself at Rubato Towers by painfully headbutting a poem in lower case.

```
loneliness by kafkaa

a poet without a muse
a poirot without any clues
a woodpecker without a tree
a bishop with nothing to see
a dove without an olive branch
a texan without a ranch
a mouse without a cheese
a belard without a loise
a bubble without a squeak a hue without a cry
a politician without a lie
a shark without a loan
a roach without a joint of his own
a gearwheel without a cog
a lumberjack without a log
a snipe without a bog
but saddest of all a flea without a dog
```

kafkaa had just settled in when Mortimer returned. He was much stouter and sleeker than when I had first met him, and affected a dressing gown of Turkestan silk left behind by his relative Terence Ratagain. Life with my neighbours had been good but had ended abruptly over a disputed Camembert. I took Mortimer's part entirely. If they had not intended him to eat it all, why did they leave it out?

By now the pandemic lockdown had started. It was no time for a mouse to be wandering about in search of a home. I let him stay, discovering his name of Mortimer for the first time. In the gloom of the pandemic, I also discovered his astonishing gift for composing inspirational homilies. Remembering the success of Hilde Marchant's celebrated "Chin-Up Corner" in the wartime Daily Express I was certain that he could find a market for his talents in the pandemic. This exquisite volume is the result, collecting Mortimer's finest maxims, each one a beautiful and unique reason to be cheerful.

kafkaa at his lower-case work

kafkaa bonded with Mortimer and committed himself to write a free verse life of mortimer to match his relative's life of mehitabel.

It was through this effort that I learnt the astonishing secrets of Mortimer's past lives. kafkaa told me why he had made little progress:

```
say boss
i hardly know where to begin
mortimer has had so many pasts
you see every mouse gets eightyone lives
because he or she is fated to meet nine cats
and is given nine lives per cat
anyway mortimer was once the court jester
for the roman emperor augustus
under the name of ridiculus mus
the emperor took him everywhere
dressed in imperial purple
but that made the previous favourite jealous
a feline called catigula
and when augustus was busy carrying on with cleopatra
catigula snuck up on him and ate him purple and all
then mortimer came back as the little mouse
who got frightened under the chair
of the first queen elizabeth
but she got mad and had him executed
when he saw her without her make-up
another time he got a big promotion in the afterlife
as the giant rat of sumatra
in the sherlock holmes case that was too scary
for doctor watson to publish
and he got a job as a stooge in the legendary showbiz
   ratpack
as the pliant rat of sinatra
and this one boss you have to believe
he was the dictator of china for some thirty years
only i found it hard to understand him
because he spoke of this in a strange
mousey tongue
```

Glorious pasts indeed. But none so glorious as his present life as the creator of this wonderful volume "Keep Squeaking Through".

Mortimer began to affect a dressing gown of Turkestan silk

The Motivational Maxims
of Mortimer Mouse

Life is just the bread in your sandwich of dreams.

The stars may be receding at the speed of light, but you can always reach Planet Content.

Be true to yourself. Your conscience has no resale value.

Lies are like lilies. The sweeter they smell, the faster they wither. But the truth is a cactus.

The hardest miles are easy if you start them with the S.

When the milk of life goes sour, be patient. Before you know, it will be cheese.

A dog barks at the Moon. Another dog joins it, and another. Soon hundreds of dogs are baying into the night. The Moon shines on and rises in the sky. When your world is full of baying dogs, be the Moon.

If you must have a deadly sin, choose sloth. Then you won't bother with the other six.

Things are never as bad as they look – only as bad as you look at them.

A man slips on a banana skin. He falls and curses. But if he had missed it and turned the corner, he would have been hit by a skidding truck.

Your past is nothing more than the first rushes of an unfinished movie. Edit it and insist on director's cut.

Somewhere in this world, a nightingale is singing to an elephant in a moonlit stream and a child is reunited with a lost puppy.

When you're in a slump, it's just life taking the chance of a little nap.

The universe is trying to send you a big package of joy, but if you're not in it will be left with a neighbour.

When life has you on your knees, plant a few crocuses while you're down there.

Somewhere at any moment, there's a very fat man in a top hat stepping on a banana skin.

Congratulations! You have been chosen for the remake of It's A Wonderful Life.

Some people can see the light at the end of the tunnel. Others put a tunnel in front of every light.

People who spend their lives in the middle of the road rarely get to the end of it.

When life leaves you in the mud, be a hippopotamus.

When your boss has you on the carpet, turn it into a magic one and fly to your enchanted place.

Why expect the worst and get bad news twice over?

When everything makes you down, be a duck!

When you see a dark cloud, be grateful that it is rain and not locusts.

Your life is a long flowing river. Don't let it be dammed – or damned.

When you see wasps heading down your way, they can only mean jam today.

When life becomes a joke, try to beat it to the punchline.

A thing worth doing is worth failing at.

To you it's a bog but to a bug it's an infinity pool.

Might is not always right, but might have been is always wrong.

When you can't see the wood for the trees, would you rather be in a desert?

Without rain there would be no rainbows.

Without the blues there would be no bluebirds.

Happy places need no visas. Your mind can just walk right in.

If you're living in the shadows that must mean there's a light somewhere.

When you get the blues, turn them into skies.

When life's driving you up the wall, take the chance to paint it.

Even when you've checked in for a long stay at Heartbreak Hotel, remember to tip the bell hop. And have you noticed how crowded it is? Why not talk to some of the other residents? Offer them the cruet in the breakfast room.

You can't grow eggs in an eggplant, but you'll grow lots of hugs in a hug plant.

Pack up your troubles in your old kit bag. Then check it into a locker and throw away the key!

Without depressions there could never be summits.

Take a minute each day to envy yourself.

Why stay in a pique when you could be climbing a peak?

Maximally motivational musings from the rodent philosopher

What I learnt at school

I went to many famous schools in my past lives. Westmouseter… Squeton… Harrodent. My eminent cousin Terence Ratagain went to that one in his time. In 1929 he opened the ratting for the school in the great match against Squeton at Hordes.

My favourite school is not nearly so well-known, but it gave me the outlook on life I have put into this book. The Nilby Mouse Academy.

The school motto was "Act for others, think for yourself."

We had a school song, "Here's Lurking At You." We had to sing it at assembly each day.

Here's lurking at you

Not shirking for you.

Good morning, dear teachers,

We're working for you.

Apart from the usual lessons there was a compulsory debating society where we learnt the art of public squeaking, and a financial class where we learnt about successful infesting.

I would recommend the school's approach to pupils to any other for any species.

Ten per cent admonition and ninety per cent admiration.

Keep some silly rules in the book to provide the thrill of breaking them.

To discover is more important than to know.

A philosopher's education

A Song with additional lyrics
by my poetic friend kafkaa

For whom would I dream	*Eb*
Or take one for the team	*Cm7*
Or work up some steam	*Cm7*
Unless it were you?	*Fm7 sus*
Unless it were you	*Fm7*

```
For whom would I care
For whom would I dare
Fight a tiger or bear
Unless it were you?
Unless it were you
```

You are the cheese on my toastie	*Fm7*
You are the cheese on my cheese	*Bb6*

```
You're my special mail from the postie    F7 Bb
You make my whole life a breeze.   F7 Bb
```

For whom would I pine
And hope for a sign
That one day you'd be mine
Unless it were you?
Unless it were you

For whom would I long
With a love that's so strong
As to beg for in song
Unless it were you?
Unless it were you.

You are the beats in my haiku
Five seven five all in threes:
I'm trying to say that I like you
Even more than my cheese.

For whom would I mope
And act like a dope
And try to soft soap
Unless it were you?
Unless it were you.

For whom would I dream
And constantly scheme
And wait for love's gleam
Unless it were you?
Unless it were you.   *Final Eb*

More maxims of mine

Life's sunspots are not really spots. They're parts of the Sun that are just a bit cooler than the rest.

If at first you don't succeed, try, try, and try again. If then you don't succeed, redefine success.

When it's too dark to see, you could try removing your sunglasses.

When you need a helping hand, walk south from your elbow.

When life is a frost, make a snowman.

When life gives you the pip, grow it into another apple tree.

Don't cry when the wind seizes your kite. It's just the sky claiming another bird.

When you can't see the silver lining, drill into your memories and do some silver mining.

When you're vulnerable, that's the best time to bring off a grand slam.

Every match has its highlights.

When you're in the soup, make it a plateful not a tureen.

When you're on the skids, get a sledge.

No matter how slippery, a slope always goes up as well as down.

From the slough of despond, it is but a short step to the windsor of majesty.

When the garden of life is filled with weeds, remember that the fuchsia lies ahead.

Any average can always improve.

The colder the night, the brighter the stars.

Be glad you have the right to be unhappy.

There is no lockdown tougher than a mind's.

Every card can be part of a winning hand. The two of clubs can sometimes beat the ace of spades.

When you miss a penalty, think of all the penalties that have missed you.

When you're going down, remember that's the fun part of the roller coaster ride.

Every pearl was once a grain of sand.

Make the present a birthday present to yourself.

Get real only when you run out of dreams.

When all else fails, do the right thing.

Every planet has its sun. There are deckchairs on Pluto.

When you're on the rocks, why not rock and roll?

When life is a turkey, that's the time for thanksgiving.

When you get that Mood Indigo, drop the D for Doom and make it Mood In I Go!

Better false dawns than real midnights.

When your soul's feeling down at heel, change into your dancing shoes.

When life deals you nothing but lemons, remember that's a winning line on a fruit machine.

You need no special training to run a four-minute smile.

To move in the best circles is as easy as π.

When misery gets too familiar, block him and seek the kindness of strangers.

We can't all be unicorns but we're all of us unique.

You are a kingdom and its soul ruler.

Better to be a merry Martian than a miserable Marchioness.

Even when you can't sleep, you can still dream.

When life takes the biscuit, remember that you still have the cup of tea.

Why be sore when you can soar?

Block the past if you don't want to take its calls, but keep the future on speed dial.

Tears are the soul's lawn sprinklers. But don't keep them running!

When life gives you the brush-off, that's the time to say "Excuse my dust!"

When life gives you hard knocks, why not open the door and say "Hi, Opportunity, I've been waiting for you"?

It's better to be weird than to be wired.

Try hope as a raft in your next flood of tears.

To put on your best face, wash it daily in hope and water.

When the clocks go back, you don't have to live in Greenwich MEAN Time. Try having a Greenwich GOOD Time.

Leaves fall that little kids and puppies may run through them.

There's enough stars to go round for everyone. Yours is up there even if you can't see it.

My answers to guilt

Why beat yourself up over your failures when so many others will do it for you?

Make guilt a trip not a daily destination. Nobody's that bad, not even you.

Sometimes you are an extra without any lines in the movie of your life.

You are not always the defendant. Sometimes you're not even an expert witness.

Don't take the blame for everything. Some of it was just the way it was.

A song from my tribute band
The Squeakch Boys (lyrics by kafkaa)

Shouldn't we be mice and all stay friendly
In a world where everybody's kind
And happy just to have a hole to live in
And a piece of cheese which isn't rind?

Life can change so fast from grim to grinning
Keep a smile and then you're always winning!

Shouldn't we be mice and stay contented,
Making every day a special prize?
There isn't any room for blues and worries
When you live in space that's just our size.

Take a lifestyle tip from good old Morti
It's OK at times to act quite naughty!
So shouldn't we be mice?

Doesn't need a lucky charm or magic spell
To make it true (dreams come true)
If you live just like a mouse you'll find
That you become one too.

We can be happy (and never get snappy)
And never feel tiny (and never get whiny).
Oh shouldn't we be mice?

So let's take a chance, we won't regret it,
A merry mousey life, let's seek to get it
And just squeak to get it.
Oh shouldn't we be mice?

My New Year Maxims

The Sun is in the Goat. So now is the time to Goatoit!

For your New Year Resolution, why not give up giving up?

Last year is SO last year.

New Year greeting

Another song with help from kafkaa

Written for the charity Chance to shine, which brings cricket to children who might not get any. Richard told me all about it.

The night may seem too dark for you to dream
But a new day is waiting there in line.
Somebody wants you in their team:
Everybody gets a chance to shine.

The rain never lasts your whole life through,
The sky will unlock and turn out fine.
So reach up and paint it red and blue:
Everybody gets a chance to shine.

There's nothing that you can't hit,
There's nothing that you can't throw,
There's nothing that you can't catch,
And nothing that you can't know.

You can squeeze the whole world inside a ball,
And stitch it very tight with thread and twine,
So catch it on the run, don't let it fall:
Everybody gets a chance to shine.

You don't always need to be so strong,
But just to use your bat in perfect time,
And watch your world-and-ball go swift and long:
Everybody gets a chance to shine.

There's nothing that you can't hit,
There's nothing that you can't throw,
There's nothing that you can't catch,
And no seed you cannot sow.

You don't have to live inside your past:
The scorer will make another sign.
So play each innings better than the last:
Everybody gets a chance to shine.

When life bowls you a fast inswinging yorker, step out and flick it to leg.

When life keeps bowling you bouncers, you can duck or hook but never retreat.

Mouse Not Out

Written for Joe Biden's Inauguration Speech

"The earth is a very small town in the giant prairie of space. We have no choice but to be good neighbors."

"America is a family and no family can thrive when a few feast at the high table and all the rest look in at the window hoping for the scraps that remain."

"We have all been stumbling on a darkened path. Let us now stop trying to trip each other up and seek to light the path together."

My major maxim, set to verse by kafkaa

'Twas the night before Christmas and in the big house
The last creature stirring was Mortimer Mouse
Devising some uplifting sentiments new
To fill up his masterpiece <u>Keep Squeaking Through:</u>
Motivational mush from a born optimist,
The book that will soon top the bestseller list.

His secret reason for keeping awake
Was trusting that Santa Claus wasn't a fake.
A message to Santa he'd sent up the flue
Asking for Wensleydale and Cornish Blue.
He knew well that Santa faced billions of pleas
But hoped he could drop in some small bits of cheese.

For hours poor Mortimer paced in the dark
As even the foxes slept on in the park,
Screechless at last in the moon's pallid light,
Their usual lovemaking stilled for this night.
One thought beat on Mortimer's soul like a drum:
Had he been too naughty for Santa to come?

At last he could hear a faint noise on the roof.
He tried to believe that it might be a hoof.
He pinned back his ears and strained hard to hear more,
But just then a note was pushed under his door.
It said "Owing to factors beyond my control
I cannot deliver now to your mousehole.
There's a terrible shortage of hauliers this year
And I've lost as many as four of my deer.
I've no bloody Dancer and no bloody Vixen
And no takeout Donner and no bloody Blitzen.
With four missing reindeer I haven't the speed
To visit each household and drop what they need.
If you give me a name I will certainly labour
To leave your request with a suitable neighbour."
The same message appeared under millions of doors
All signed "Yours regretfully, (Mr) S Claus."

Poor Mortimer sniffled but did not repine.
He took up his pen and wrote a new line
Of uplifting thought for his uplifting book.
He stiffened his sinews and told himself "Look,
Things could be much worse when the times are like these.
If Santa can't visit, I'll make my own cheese."

And this is what Mortimer wrote with a smile
(The King's Christmas message could learn from his style):

The sky may be dark but it still is the sky
And it's waiting there for you if you choose to fly.
So soar like an eagle and don't be a grouse

Signed, Yours very truly
Mortimer Mouse.

A message from Mortimer Mouse

Thank you, thank you, for reading this book. If even one of my little maxims made your life better it makes mine better too.

I am always glad to have new suggestions for maxims and illustrations for my next book.

Do send them to me at mortimailcheese@gmail.com

Visit my website www.mortimermouse.co.uk if you would like a print or T-shirt or other merchandise with the illustration and maxim of your choice.

Please tell me your age if you are under 18.

Mortimer

About the Editor

Mortimer's editor Richard Heller is the author of *The Prisoner Of Rubato Towers*, published by Xerus Publishing, which tells the story of his dramatic meeting with Mortimer and of their early life together. He has also written two cricket novels *A Tale Of Ten Wickets* and *The Network*. With Peter Oborne he wrote *White On Green*, celebrating the drama of Pakistan cricket, and they present a regular cricket-themed podcast. In past lives he was a long-serving humorous columnist on *The Mail On Sunday* and worked in the movie business in the United States and the UK. This included a brief engagement on a motion picture called *Cycle Sluts Versus The Zombie Ghouls*. Before that he was chief of staff to Denis Healey, then Deputy Leader of the Labour Party, and later to Gerald Kaufman, then Shadow Home Secretary. He has also twice been a finalist on BBC Television's *Mastermind*.

About the Illustrator

Mortimer's illustrator, **Amina Art Ansari** is a British-Pakistani visual artist born in London. Her rich academic journey includes studies at Central Saint Martins, London College of Printing, and the National College of Arts in Lahore, Pakistan. She has rendered portraits of Quaid-e-Azam Mohd Ali Jinnah for the Pakistan High Commission in London, as well as Her Majesty Queen Elizabeth II and the Duke of Edinburgh in Windsor Castle. Amina's artistic influence extends beyond canvas; she has conducted Art Workshops aboard HMS Argyll of the Royal Navy and at Lord's Cricket Ground, MCC. Her evocative British Army painting earned prominence at the Ministry of Defence's unveiling. She has won numerous awards for art and public speaking and various media have covered her work including the BBC. Moreover, her resilience shines through as she recently underwent cochlear implant surgery. Amina's multifaceted character encompasses a background in Fine Arts, event management, and communication direction and she has built a huge network from fashion, media, cultural domains.

https://aminaartansari.com

Amina Art Ansari by herself